HAUNTED COPPER COUNTRY

The History & Ghost Stories of Michigan's Keweenaw Peninsula

LISA A. SHIEL

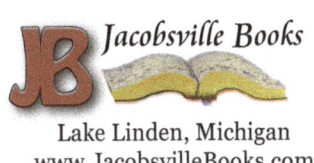

Jacobsville Books

Lake Linden, Michigan
www.JacobsvilleBooks.com

HAUNTED COPPER COUNTRY
Copyright © 2014 by Lisa A. Shiel
All rights reserved.
First paperback edition 2015.

Cover art by Kerrie Shiel & Lisa A. Shiel
Used by permission.

No portion of this book may be copied, reproduced, or transmitted in any form or by any means, electronic or otherwise, including recording, photocopying, or inclusion in any information storage and retrieval system, without the express written permission of the publisher and author, except for brief excerpts quoted in published reviews.

ISBN: 978-1-934631-53-9 (pbk.)
ISBN: 978-1-934631-49-2 (e-book: EPUB)
LCCN: 2015934026

Manufactured in the United States.

Jacobsville Books
www.JacobsvilleBooks.com
1-866-341-3705

    Publisher's Cataloging-in-Publication Data
       provided by Five Rainbows Services

Shiel, Lisa A.
  Haunted Copper Country : the history & ghost stories of Michigan's Keweenaw Peninsula / Lisa A. Shiel.
    pages cm
  ISBN: 978-1-934631-49-2 (e-book: EPUB)
  1. Ghosts—Michigan. 2. Haunted places—Michigan . 3. Michigan—History. 4. Upper Peninsula (Mich.)—History, Local.   I. Title.
BF1472.U6 S525 2014
133.109`774—dc23

                                      2015934026

THE KEWEENAW PENINSULA

Map courtesy of the University of Texas Libraries, the University of Texas at Austin

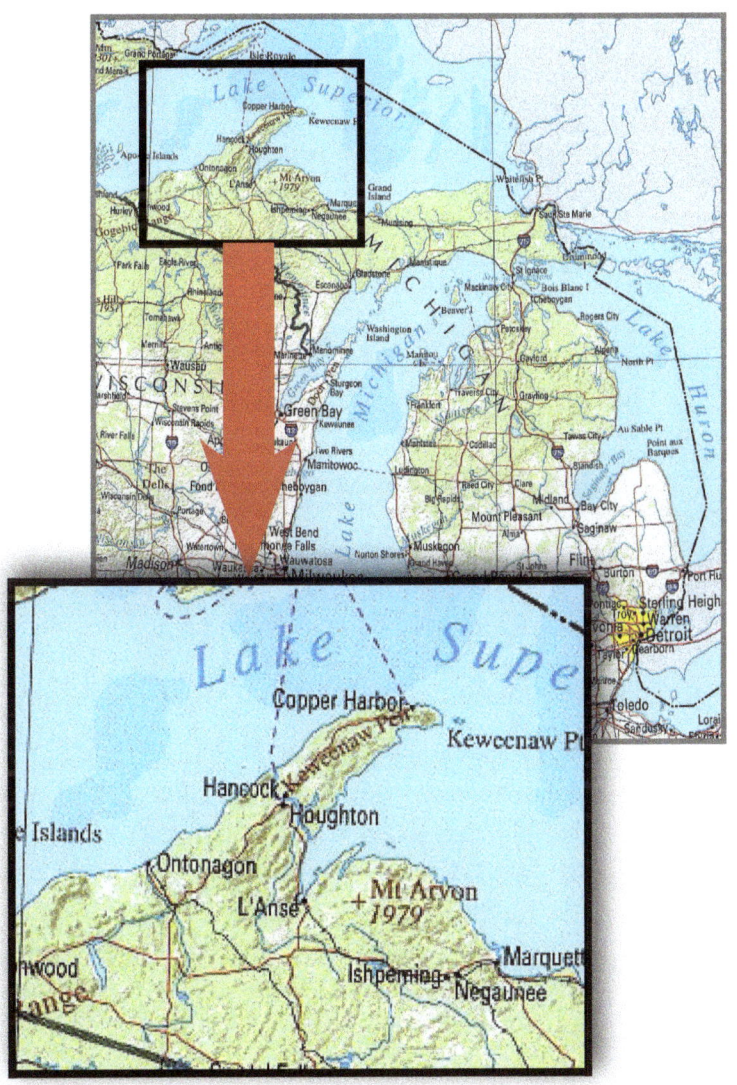

Other Books by Lisa A. Shiel

Fiction

From Jacobsville Books

Confronting Sasquatch
Faces of Bigfoot **[e-book]**
Faces of Bigfoot 2 **[e-book]**
The Faces of Bigfoot Collection **[e-book]**

The Human Origins Series
The Hunt for Bigfoot (Book One)
Lord of the Dead (Book Two)
Relic of the Ancient Ones (Book Three)
Revenge of the Ancient Ones (Book Four)
Bigfoot Beginnings (Backstories, Vol. 1) **[e-book]**
The Bigfoot Effect (Backstories, Vol. 2) **[e-book]**
Traces of Bigfoot (Backstories, Vol. 1& 2) **[e-book]**
Bigfoot, Mummies, and Aliens: The Human Origins Series Collection (Books 1-4 with Backstories Vol. 1 &2) **[e-book]**

Nonfiction

From Jacobsville Books

Forbidden Bigfoot
Creature of Controversy (Forbidden Bigfoot, Part One) **[e-book]**
Top Secret Sasquatch (Forbidden Bigfoot, Part Two) **[e-book]**
Backyard Phenomena (Forbidden Bigfoot, Part Three) **[e-book]**
The Evolution Conspiracy
Backyard Bigfoot

From The History Press

Forgotten Tales of Michigan's Upper Peninsula

From Trails Books

Strange Michigan (with Linda S. Godfrey)

CONTENTS

The Keweenaw Peninsula iii
Other Books by Lisa A. Shiel iv

Acknowledgments...vii
Introduction ix

Chapter One: Calumet 1
  Red Metal Days 1
  The Making of Ghosts 8
    December Disaster..8
    Ghosts of the Hall 12
  The Calumet Theatre 14
    Dramatic Spirits 17
  The Calumet Colosseum 21
    Frozen Spirits.. 24

Chapter Two: Laurium 27
  A Checkered Past 27
    The Captain's House... 31
    Ghosts of the Manor 34

Chapter Three: Kearsarge 36
  A Booming History 36
    The Osceola Effect 37
    Kearsarge, Ahoy! 39
    Phantoms of a Boom Town 44

Chapter Four: Jacobsville 49
  A Rocky Past 50
  Spirits of the Past 56
    The Old Strawberry Farm 56
    The Spurned Husband 59
    Hairy Ghosts 60
    Spirit Orbs 62

References 65

ACKNOWLEDGMENTS

I'D LIKE TO TAKE THIS OPPORTUNITY TO THANK THE FOLKS WHO GRACIOUSLY OF- fered their knowledge and support to me during the writing of this book. I'm grateful to all of them:

- John Grathoff of Calumet Paranormal—https://www.facebook.com/pages/Calumet-Paranormal/232934792572
- Jenny Rohlf and Lori Brown Smith of Keweenaw Paranormal Society—https://www.facebook.com/groups/597334596991088/

Please check out their Facebook pages. They've done some fascinating work investigating the haunted side of the Copper Country.

INTRODUCTION

For as long as humans have sat around campfires in the dark of night, we have told spooky stories to entertain and unsettle each other. The human affinity for fear, under controlled circumstances, is nothing new. We love to be scared. Scientists may come up with biological and sociological reasons for this love of getting spooked, but all that really matters is that we do enjoy a good thrill. Ghost stories have always played a significant role in our need for controlled fear.

Does this mean ghosts aren't real? Of course not. Millions of people around the world believe in life after death, and that spirits communicate with the living (or at least try to) for various reasons ranging from unfinished business to comforting loved ones left behind. The purpose of this book is not to debate these beliefs, or to prove whether ghosts do indeed exist. This book has one purpose—to serve as a textual campfire around which you, the reader, may huddle to immerse yourself in some of the spookiest tales from Michigan's Copper Country.

Unless you live in Michigan, you may not have heard of the Copper Country, also known as the Keweenaw Peninsula. It lies on the northwestern end of the Upper Peninsula, near Wisconsin, and it juts out across Lake Superior toward Canada. The Keweenaw has an ancient and mysterious history, beginning with its formation from the remnants of a prehistoric rift valley. The region's volatile geologic past led to the creation of its most famous natural resource—copper. A genuine earthquake happened nearby back in 2010, just outside the southern U.P. town of Escanaba. Maybe the region's history of quaking and shaking keeps the spirits unsettled. Whatever the reason, the Copper Country boasts a surprising number of haunted places for such a small area.

This book is more than a collection of ghost stories. It's also a celebration of the Copper Country's rich and diverse history. Because I live and write here in the heart of the Keweenaw, I have developed a deep appreciation for and fascination with the region's history—and its paranormal side. In my previous book, *Forgotten Tales of Michigan's Upper Peninsula*, I presented little-known stories from the Keweenaw's mining heyday in the 1800s and early 1900s, everything from strange murders to unexplained earth tremors. In *Haunted Copper Country*, I delve into even stranger stories involving close encounters of the otherworldly kind. Each haunted tale is woven into the historical background of the location in question, offering a fuller picture of what makes a haunted place, because behind every ghost story is a true story. Sometimes the truth is merely a seed out of which tales grow; in other cases, the history overshadows the ghostly goings-on. This book endeavors to shed light on both types of haunted tales, from well-known hauntings to stories never before published.

Is the Copper Country haunted? Read these tales and decide for yourself.

CHAPTER ONE
CALUMET

IN HOUGHTON COUNTY, JUST NORTH OF THE CITIES OF HOUGHTON AND HANCOCK, lies the high country—a gathering of communities nestled atop the spine of the Keweenaw, in an area prone to heavy snowfalls. Today, Calumet Township includes the villages of Calumet and Laurium, plus the surrounding communities of Osceola, Centennial Heights, and Kearsarge. These days, no one would consider Calumet to be a bustling metropolis, but in the heyday of copper mining, Calumet was just such a place.

RED METAL DAYS

By the 1860s, Calumet had already become well established as a copper mining community, and in 1866 a new road was under construction that would connect Calumet Township with Hancock to the south. The operations of the Calumet & Hecla Mining Company, often known simply as C&H, served as the impetus for much of the development in the Calumet area. Back in those days, however, Calumet was known as Red Jacket—and the village now called Laurium was known as Calumet. This makes the history of the region a bit confusing at times, especially since Red Jacket was often known colloquially as Calumet. The two villages of Red Jacket and Calumet (Laurium) existed side-by-side, much as they do today. When driving up M-26 from Lake Linden, it's hard to distinguish the modern villages of Laurium and Calumet, as their boundaries blend together.

Back in the days when Calumet was Red Jacket and Laurium was Calumet, the township that encompassed both villages boasted an ethnically diverse population. Finnish, Cornish,

Copper played once served as the keystone of Calumet's economy. This monument preserves a chunk of float copper weighing in at 9,392 pounds, which was dug up a few miles outside the village back in 1970. Photo by Lisa A. Shiel.

Irish, and Italian immigrants are most famous today for the part they played in Calumet's history, but Houghton County also became home to immigrants of Croatian, Chinese, French Canadian, Polish, and Slovenian descent. By 1870, Calumet Township supported 3,182 residents, with immigrants making up over 60% of the population. At this time, the village of Calumet (now Laurium) had yet to be born.

The year 1875 marked a milestone in the township's history, as Red Jacket became an incorporated village. By this time, the township had five schools and library with over five hundred books, making it the largest library in the Keweenaw. The township's population continued to grow at a brisk pace, thanks in large part to C&H and other local mining operations. As of 1880, the population had surged to 8,299 in the township as a whole, with 2,140 of those residents in Red Jacket. Copper mining had reached its boom, and things would only get better, economically speaking, for the next three decades. Mining was hard and dangerous work, but copper made the Keweenaw. Without it, Calumet might never have reached the heights it achieved during the days of C&H.

The 1880s found the township expanding again and again. A town hall was built in 1886, and in 1889 the village of Calumet emerged southeast of Red Jacket. Six years later, the new village underwent a name change to officially become Laurium, the name that has endured since. Meanwhile, Red Jacket had grown to such size and prosperity that a Marquette newspaper dubbed it "the most cosmopolitan town in America." Since many of Red Jacket's businesses boasted electric lights and other modern amenities, the moniker seems well deserved. By 1898, the village of Red Jacket had swelled to over 4,000 residents, with another 30,000 in the communities that surrounded it. Calumet Township had become one of the largest metropolises in the state. Perhaps this explains why a there's a long-standing myth that Calumet was once in the running for the title of state capital. Although no one has found proof to support the state capital rumor, it does stand as further evidence of what a thriving community Calumet Township had become.

During the copper boom, the Keweenaw—and especially Calumet Township—developed into a flourishing economy. In 1899, C&H reported stock dividends of $10 million. Taking inflation into account, in 2014 those dividends would equate to approximately $278 million. That's an impressive profit for any company in today's world of multinational corporations. Back in 1899, it was staggering, particularly considering that C&H was one company that operated solely in the Keweenaw and mined nothing but copper. No wonder immigrants flooded to the Copper Country in

The interior of the Quincy Mine, now a tourist destination but once a powerhouse of copper production. The mine sits between Hancock and Calumet. Photo by Lisa A. Shiel.

pursuit of their own American dreams. Mining may have been thankless work that claimed many lives, and the Keweenaw's climate and remoteness may have pushed pioneers to the breaking point and beyond, but the region certainly offered bountiful opportunities for those brave enough to take up the challenge. The individuals who owned and ran the mining operations saw the most profit, naturally, and a growing sense of unrest would lead to a defining moment in Calumet's history.

In the meantime, however, the township kept on growing. The turn of the century saw a population of some 45,000 residents living within three miles of Red Jacket and Laurium. Two years into the new century, the township welcomed trolley service, thanks to the Houghton County Traction Company and its new line that ran from Houghton all the way up to Mohawk, north of Calumet, with stops in the township. In 1910, residents throughout Houghton County voted to create the Houghton County Road Commission, which maintains the area's roadways to this day.

Then came 1913. For the Copper Country, this year would turn out to be infamous.

The story of C&H begins in 1858, when surveyor and amateur geologist Edwin J. Hulbert uncovered a vast treasure—the Calumet conglomerate lode, a rich copper-bearing deposit that extended from Portage Lake all the way up to the Eagle River area. This portion of the Keweenaw's copper deposits proved the most valuable of all. Hulbert, with the financial support of investors, started the Hulbert Mining Company. Soon, the company purchased the land that contained the Calumet conglomerate and created subsidiaries, the Calumet Mining Company and the Hecla Mining Company. Eventually, the companies merged to become the Calumet & Hecla Mining Company, and under the management of Alexander Agassiz C&H would become a powerhouse. By the 1870s, C&H boasted a workforce of over 5,000 and shipped out over 80 million pounds of copper every year. At one point, C&H was the most productive copper mining company in the world.

The company's policy of corporate paternalism—essentially treating its workers like children, with C&H as the parent—worked for decades. C&H became highly profitable and its policies helped nurture a thriving local economy. Instead of running company stores, C&H allowed businesses to grow up naturally, to serve the needs of the growing labor force. At the same time, C&H either gave workers homes to live in or provided land on which they could build houses. The tactic was meant to encourage families, and therefore a stable environment for their workers, rather than the bawdy lifestyle common to mining communities of the era.

Agassiz, though without doubt a skilled manager, adopted one particular policy that fostered tensions between C&H and its workers. He was staunchly anti-union. C&H's anti-union stance served only to increase the discontent brewing among the workers. As the company and the workforce burgeoned, the workers saw their relationship with management change from one of personal contact to a more detached affiliation. And of course, the language barrier grew taller as more and more non-English speakers entered the C&H workforce. Corporate paternalism was stretched to its limit as the family swelled larger and larger.

Labor problems first emerged in the 1880s, with small strikes, and tensions rose ever higher as the years passed, especially when the Western Federation of Miners (WFM) came to region in 1908 to court the workers. Miners blew up nitroglycerin in protests against the use of the explosive. But these scuffles would prove trivial in comparison to the summer of 1913. When C&H made public their plans to switch to one-man drills, a move that would cut numerous jobs, workers banded together—and with the help of WFM—they went on strike. C&H's mining operations went dark.

C&H, under the direction of Agassiz, refused to back down on their anti-union stance or on the one-man drills. These weren't the only grievances the workers voiced. Safety was a top concern, and an ongoing problem, for all the mining op-

A statue of Alexander Agassiz sits outside the old C&H library, now part of the Keweenaw National Historic Park. Photo by Lisa A. Shiel.

erations. In just one year, 1911, sixty-three workers had died in the mines. In 1912, more than forty workers died and over six hundred were seriously injured. The one-man drills not only reduced the workforce, but brought greater danger, since a man working a drill alone would have nobody to call for help. With all the dangers, and C&H's anti-union mindset, perhaps the strike should've come as no surprise to C&H. After all, despite the company's anti-union actions, by 1913 at least 2,000 workers belonged to unions.

A letter from the WFM to various mining companies found no traction, as officials outright refused to meet with the union or the workers. On July 23, 1913, the strike began—shutting down every mine in the Keweenaw, including C&H.

Violence erupted on both sides, sporadically. In an unprovoked attack that would go down in history as an egregious injustice, a half dozen men from a detective agency fired a hail of bullets into a boardinghouse south of Houghton, killing two men. Four of the shooters were convicted of manslaughter, another was acquitted, and the last man was reportedly whisked away to New York by C&H officials, where he served as a spy. At least one other shooting would follow, with a fourteen-year-old girl as the victim and no punishment for the perpetrator.

Strikers were chased, beaten, and generally terrorized by vigilantes working for the mining companies. This vigilantes called themselves the Citizens' Alliance. By December 1913, the atmosphere of rage and fear would climax with a tragedy that echoes down the halls of Calumet's history to this day.

THE MAKING OF GHOSTS

What causes spirits to linger after death? This question has never found a definitive answer, and probably never will find one. People often speculate that unfinished business may keep some spirits grounded, while other ghosts may stem from great tragedies that trigger a sort of spiritual reverberation. These echoes lead to hauntings. In the case of Calumet's Italian Hall, the latter explanation seems likely.

DECEMBER DISASTER

The Italian Hall, created by the Italian Mutual Benefit Society, served as a meeting place for mine workers and their families. When the hall opened in 1889, C&H's general manager spoke at the grand opening festivities. In December 1913, the striking workers and their families gathered at the Hall on Christmas Eve for a children's Christmas party. The crowd included over five hundred children and nearly two hundred adults. Eyewitnesses reported that a man wearing a button identifying him as a member of the Citizens' Alliance rushed up the stairs to the second floor and cried, "Fire!"

Men, women, and children stampeded for the exits. Some have speculated that a few members of the fleeing mob tripped on the fifth step on the stairs. Whatever the cause, someone fell—and the domino effect brought down one after another, body after body, in a crushing pile-up that would kill upwards of seventy people—including as many as sixty children. As the panic escalated, children tumbled into a mass at the foot of the stairs and could not claw free, weighed down by the weight of their own bodies and those of the adults who got caught in the crush. Upstairs, at least a few children managed to escape through a second-story window with the help of a ladder. Although the exact death toll is unknown, thanks to the inefficient methods of reporting such tragedies in that era, no one disputes that at least several dozen died that night. The tragedy captured the attention of the entire nation. *The Miner's Bulletin* included this account, which epitomizes the horror of the Italian Hall disaster:

> "One little girl who was jammed in the hallway in a dying condition begged one of her rescuers to save her. She grasped his hand, kissed it, then her little head dropped upon her breast and she was dead."

Recently, historians claim to have uncovered evidence that the Italian Hall disaster was not an accident, but rather the culmination of months of escalating terrorism and violence on the part of C&H and the other mining companies. Whether the man who started the panic in the Italian Hall worked for C&H or simply approved of its tactics, no one really knows. He may have been a vigilante working for C&H who decided to take matters into his own hands. Whatever the case, the actions of C&H and its cohort companies undoubtedly played a key role in the deaths at the Italian Hall, if only by fostering an atmosphere of militant opposition to the strike. At the time, many people blamed the Citizens Alliance, as made clear in a political cartoon published in a local Finnish newspaper. The cartoon shows Death himself hovering over the caskets of the dead carrying a banner that reads "Citizens Alliance."

Meanwhile, WFM president Charles Moyer seemed to take advantage of the disaster in a callous effort to further the union cause. On the night of the tragedy, as bodies were still being removed from the Hall, Moyer wired President Woodrow Wilson and other officials demanding an immediate investigation into the event. Then the day after the tragedy, Moyer issued a statement in which he claimed an outsider had started the panic, a

The archway is all that remains of the Italian Hall. A historical marker offers testament to the tragedy, and plaques affixed to the columns memorialize the dead. Photo by Lisa A. Shiel.

The Italian Hall as it looked the morning after the fire. This historic photo appears on a pedestal at the memorial site. Photo by Lisa A. Shiel.

statement that may explain where the rumor originated. Even today, no one knows for certain what happened or how many people died that night.

Moyer didn't stop there, though. In the days after the tragedy, he turned down money donated by locals who wanted to help. The funds amounted to thousands of dollars that might've aided survivors and helped pay for burials for the victims. A group of enraged citizens formed their own vigilante mob to hunt down Moyer, beating and shooting him. Moyer survived the attack, but made claims that C&H general manager James MacNaughton had instigated the attack. Later, Moyer recanted his claim of MacNaughton's involvement. It seems that both sides in the miners' strike would use any means necessary to win the battle. In the end, C&H would be victorious. On April 12, 2014, the workers voted by an overwhelming margin to terminate the strike.

C&H kept mining copper ore into the 1960s, although the company never again reached the heights it had achieved in its heyday.

GHOSTS OF THE HALL

Sites of tragedies, where many people died, often inspire stories of ghosts haunting the locations. Italian Hall has proved no exception. Over the years, rumors have circulated that speak of spirits inhabiting the place where once the Hall stood. Now, a monument to the tragedy—consisting of the original building's archway and a plaque—stands in place of the building.

Plaques like this one adorn the columns of the Italian Hall archway, the sole remains of the building. Photo by Lisa A. Shiel.

People visiting the site have reported feeling a presence there. A ghost hunting team from Calumet Paranormal, led by John Grathoff, visited the site late one night to check out the claims. A sandstone archway—once the doorway of the Italian Hall—stands as the only physical remnant of the disaster. Plaques mounted on the archway pillars offer prayers and calls to arms. "Sleep in heavenly peace," reads one. Another admonishes, "Mourn for the dead; Fight for the living." A brick path leads through the archway, and then circles around sandstone benches and a historical marker.

John and his team arrived around midnight and proceeded past the archway to the benches, where they sat down to wait. They set up their K2 EMF meter so that everyone could see it. Because this meter detects electromagnetic fields through a wide range of frequencies, ghost hunters often employ it in their investigations. The idea is that ghosts create spikes in EMF, which meters like the K2 will detect. When the meter senses a change in EMF, lights flash on its face, alerting the ghost hunters that something is happening. On this night, as John and his team sat among the ruins of the Italian Hall, their K2 meter stayed quiet, its power light glowing steadily. John compared the atmosphere that evening to sitting in his living room at home.

As they often do, the team decided to try an EVP session. EVP stands for electronic voice phenomena, and it refers to voices heard on an audio recording that were not heard at the time the recording was made. A member of John's team asked, "Is anyone with us?" The K2 meter did not flash. No one in the group heard a response. The night remained quiet and dark as the team waited in the shadow of the archway. When nothing happened, the team headed home.

Later, they listened to the recording they had made that night and discovered something that would send shivers down anyone's spine. On the recording, after the team member asked if anyone was there, a voice could be heard replying, "We are all here." The voice sounded like a child.

Could the spirits of the dozens of children who died in the disaster haunt the site today? Might one of them have responded to the ghost hunter's question? If great tragedies can trigger hauntings, then the Italian Hall disaster certainly qualifies. More than a tragedy, the events of Christmas Eve 1913 remain mysterious in many respects. Who shouted "fire"? How many died? Do their spirits live on at the site?

Questions abound. Answers are elusive.

THE CALUMET THEATRE

In 1898, the village council of Red Jacket realized their township lacked a crucial element necessary for any civilized city. They needed a real opera house. The council voted to construct a new, modern opera house to replace the Red Jacket Opera House, which resided on the second floor of the village hall. Maybe the Marquette newspaper's heralding of the Calumet area as "the most cosmopolitan town in America" had something to do with the council's decision. After all, how could they live up to such a moniker without a true opera house? Either way, two years after receiving the high praise, Red Jacket implemented a plan to construct a new opera house.

Within hours of the vote, the council contacted architect Charles Shand of Detroit to garner his participation in the project. Shand was told to spare no expense in designing the new opera house. How could anyone put a price on elegance and sophistication? By year's end, construction had begun on the Calumet Theatre. The village hall would be expanded to accommodate the new opera house. Within two years, the Theatre was finished at the discount price of $71,000—the equivalent nearly $2 million today. At the time, the Theatre stood as the only municipal opera house in the country. Everyone waited for opening night, anxious to see what their tax dollars had bought. Would the opera house live up to its hype?

THE CALUMET THEATRE

The Calumet Theatre, as it looks today. Located in downtown Calumet, it's a must-see for every tourist. Photo by Lisa A. Shiel.

On March 20, 1900, the Calumet Theatre opened for business. Twelve hundred people turned up on opening night, filling the house to capacity, despite the high ticket prices. For its grand opening performance, the Theatre hosted the operetta *The Highwayman*, written for Broadway by Reginal de Koven. The Calumet & Hecla Mining Company orchestra provided the music for the evening. Patrons raved about the architecture, the murals, and of course, the entertainment. Five grand murals spread across the vaulted ceiling illustrated the concepts of painting, music, drama, poetry, and sculpture. Above their heads, patrons glimpsed a globe-shaped chandelier constructed from copper and equipped with over a hundred electric light bulbs. The chandelier, along with a copper roof, served as a nod to the importance of red metal mining in the region. A glorious clock tower, capped with a bell tower, occupied one corner of the building.

After such a successful opening night, it might seem hard for an opera house to keep up the momentum, but the Calumet Theatre did just that. Theatrical royalty made pilgrimages to the Theatre to perform before star-struck audiences. Famous names over the years included Lillian Russell, Helena Modjeska, Sarah Bernhardt, Douglas Fairbanks, and Lon Chaney. The renowned composer and marching-band leader John Philip Sousa, dubbed the March King, also appeared at the opera house.

The mining strike of 1913-14 took a heavy toll on the opera house, as attendance plummeted in the wake of the strike itself and of the unspeakable tragedy at the Italian Hall. The opera house even served as a makeshift morgue for the bodies removed from the ruins of the Hall. Never again would the Calumet Theatre regain its standing as one of the preeminent opera houses in the nation. The year 1918 brought more bad news for the Theatre. First, Copper Country succumbed to an outbreak of the infamous Spanish flu that swept through the nation in that year. The epidemic shut down the Theatre. Then, just weeks after the opera house reopened, a fire broke out after someone left a cigarette burning in the backstage area. The beautiful copper chandelier was destroyed.

The fire marked the end of the Theatre's glory days. By the 1930s, the opera house functioned chiefly as a movie theater and would continue in that capacity well into the 1950s. In 1958, summer stock returned to the Theatre, marking the end of professional theater's three-decade absence from the opera house. The Calumet Theatre would bid farewell to summer stock a decade later. By 1971 the Theatre, now leased from the village by the Copper Country Intermediate School District, achieved landmark status—literally—when the National Park Service granted the Theatre the status of National Historic Landmark. Over the subsequent decades, the Calumet Theatre would undergo multiple efforts at renovation and restoration. The murals would be restored to their original glory; the chandelier, however, would not be recreated. The lack of photographic documentation for the copper chandelier's appearance has prohibited any reconstruction.

THE CALUMET THEATRE

The main doors of the Calumet Theatre. Photo by Lisa A. Shiel.

In 1993, the Theatre became a Heritage Site in the Keweenaw National Historic Park, a unit that spans multiple locations through the Keweenaw, from Copper Harbor to south of Houghton. Today, the Theatre once again hosts dramatic and musical performances, thanks to visiting artists and the Calumet Players, a community theater group. Performances and self-guided tours of the landmark draw in about 20,000 visitors each year.

But some people say the Theatre hosts visitors of another kind as well—the kind who should've left long ago but refuse to depart. They are the spirits of the opera house.

DRAMATIC SPIRITS

The Calumet Theatre's past is as dramatic as many of the performances visitors have enjoyed there. Mass deaths (possibly mass murder), a pandemic, a fire—this building has enough tragedy and destruction in its past to warrant a slew of hauntings. And, as it turns out, many people believe the Theatre is home to several ghosts. According to local ghost hunters, the current management refutes claims the building has any spooks. Their denials have done nothing to quell the stories.

The best-known ghost that purportedly resides in the Theatre belongs to a Polish actress named Helena Modjeska. According to the website of the Helena Modjeska Society, the madame became the most well-known actress in the United States during the nineteenth century. She excelled at Shakespearean roles—

Madame Helena Modjeska. Image courtesy of the Library of Congress, Prints & Photographs Division, LC-USZ62-99177.

which give any actress the chance to sink her teeth into dramatic and haunted characters, as well as the occasional comedic part, penned by the immortal bard. These haunted characters may have inspired the lady herself to linger after death. She has been quoted as saying, "It is a hundred times better to suffer and live than to remain asleep." Maybe she took the saying a bit farther, deciding to live on after shedding the mortal coil. Modjeska's portrait hangs in the Calumet Theatre, a testament to her fame back in the glory days of the opera house. Modjeska died in 1909 at the age of 48, and although she died in California, tales of her afterlife surround the Calumet Theatre.

Legend says that whenever her portrait is removed from the wall, inexplicable things happen inside the Theatre. Lights go out and come back on of their own volition. Strange banging and crashing sounds erupt elsewhere in the building, but investigation reveals no source for the noises. Others have felt chills from mysterious breezes inside the building, while still others insist they've heard eerie melodies echoing through the halls of the historic opera house, despite finding no source for the music.

The madame herself has made guest appearances before various people, startling them with fleeting glimpses of the elegant, dramatic lady. During the summer of 1958, the Calumet Theatre hosted a production of Shakespeare's *The Taming of the Shrew*, with an actress named Adysse Lane playing the lead role of Kate. In the midst of a vital soliloquy—a lengthy monologue that relies on one actor's performance to drive the scene forward—Lane abruptly lost her place in the script. At a loss for words, unable to recall the lines, in desperation she resorted to waving her hands about in gestures she prayed would distract the audience from her sudden silence. Whether the tactic worked or not is hard to gauge, but Lane valiantly struggled to keep her performance going.

Just when the actress thought she'd blown the entire scene, and would have to walk off the stage in disgrace, Lane felt an unknown force raising her hand. The otherworldly power lifted her arm until her hand pointed at an area on the Theatre's second balcony where, behind a spotlight, she glimpsed the figure of a woman. It was, Lane claimed, none other than Madame Helena Modjeska. By this time, the audience may well have wondered about Lane's unusual performance of the scene. But as the living actress watched her long-departed counterpart on the balcony, Modjeska mouthed the lines for the soliloquy, thus rescuing the forgetful damsel from a very embarrassing distress. Lane got a good enough look at the spirit to describe Modjeska's dark eyes and fair skin.

A reporter from the Houghton newspaper once spent a night in the opera house in hopes of meeting Madame Modjeska in person. The reporter sat in the performance hall reading a book, by the eerie light of the exit sign, hoping for a glimpse of Modjeska herself. As the night wore on, the reporter began to wonder if anything interesting would happen, or if this would go down in history as yet another average night in a spooky old building. In an effort to encourage the ghost—or ghosts, as the case may be—the young woman walked to the portrait of Modjeska, carefully removed it from the wall, and set it down on the floor leaning against the table that stands below the spot where the portrait normally hangs. Messing with the portrait is, according to legend, one thing sure to rile up the Shakespearean ghost.

The reporter then returned to the theater proper and sat down to write an article on her laptop computer. A water bottle rested atop the nearby piano, on its closed lid. Suddenly, the bottle toppled over and rolled across the piano lid as if someone had touched it—but no one had. The reporter set the bottle upright again, and resumed typing. Had the water bottle fallen due to a draft or a freak vibration in the floor?

As the reporter grew more and more sleepy, she kept thinking she caught glimpses of something in the balcony, but a second glance always revealed emptiness there. Then, just when the reporter was getting ready to leave, she heard the sound of heavy breathing emanating from the rear of the hall. The breathing noise drew closer and closer, but seemed to dissipate the nearer it came to the young woman. Finally, the sound faded away altogether. Uncertain about what had happened, the reporter fled the Theater. Had she encountered one of the resident ghosts? No one can say for certain, but the reporter was not the first or the last to report an unexplained incident while visiting the landmark.

The paranormal history of the Theatre, although disputed by management, tells of other ghosts besides Madame Modjeska. Witnesses have reported hearing tortured screams reverberating through the building, and some believe the screams belong to Elanda Rowe. The legend speaks of the little girl dying at the hands of murderer on the very grounds where the Calumet Theatre now stands. Murders, especially of children, provide the backdrop for many hauntings.

Another spectral story involving the Calumet Theatre revolves around yet another reported murder. This crime took place, the story goes, back in 1903 when an adult male was killed on the grounds of the opera house. As with Elanda Rowe, this ghost screams in the dead of night, reliving his horrific death.

The only apparition of a person verified to have both lived and died is Helena Modjeska, and no one knows why she might choose to haunt the Calumet Theatre, considering how many other theaters she visited during her illustrious career. Elanda Rowe and the unnamed man remain ghosts in life as well as death, with little known about the veracity of the murder tales. What we do know is this—multiple witnesses have reported unnatural goings-on at the Calumet Theatre, a place haunted by real tragedies as well as legendary ghost stories.

THE CALUMET COLOSSEUM

Where did professional hockey get its start? In the Copper Country, of course. Canada may like to claim hockey as its proprietary sport, but the professional version of the ice game had its beginnings in the Keweenaw Peninsula of Michigan, where locals formed the first professional hockey league back in 1904. Although the league lasted just three years, dying out in 1907, it stands as the first of its kind. Today, hockey is still a big deal in the Copper Country, and teams battle for supremacy of the ice in the Calumet Colosseum. But the Colosseum hasn't always been an ice rink. Its varied past may explain why the building seems to host at least a few spirits—not of the sort imbibed by hockey fans to celebrate their team's victory, but of the deceased kind.

The Colosseum was built in 1913 as a hockey rink, and the following year saw the first game played on its ice. The headquarters of the Calumet & Hecla Mining Company lay right across the street from the Colosseum. Miners even helped out with the construction of the rink by lending a hand during installation of the artificial ice.

By 1942, however, the rink had been sold to the State of Michigan. A fire had destroyed the National Guard armory

The Calumet Colosseum. Photo by Lisa A. Shiel.

in Calumet, so the government needed a new base for the Guard's operations. An addition tacked onto the back of Colosseum provided space for the armory. Even while the building served the National Guard, the Calumet Hockey Association leased the rink during each hockey season, from October through April. Then, in 2005, Calumet Township reclaimed the Colosseum by striking a deal with state—in exchange for ownership of the building, the township would grant the state twelve acres of land on which they could build a brand-new armory.

A million dollars in improvements have spiffed up the Colosseum, but care has been taken to retain the historical character of the building. Today, the Colosseum stands as the oldest continually operated hockey rink in North America. The building even hosts the International Frisbee Hall of Fame, and it also includes a ballroom on the second floor of the armory addition. With a history of military and civilian use, it's no wonder the Colosseum houses ghosts.

The main doors of the Calumet Colosseum. Photo by Lisa A. Shiel.

FROZEN SPIRITS

Ghosts often seem to be frozen in a particular time and place, reliving tragic events or simply hanging around after death. The Calumet Colosseum, like many historic buildings, has apparently become home to its own spirits frozen in time. Over the years, visitors have reported multiple phenomena—from a disembodied voice humming circus music to glimpses of "shadow people" (dark, shadow-like figures with no discernible features). John Grathoff and the Calumet Paranormal team have visited the Colosseum on more than one occasion to investigate the claims of ghostly activity.

During one visit, the team heard a disembodied voice whistling circus music as well as the sound of a radio playing, though no radio was found. During another investigation, the team had some truly spooky experiences in the Colosseum. A group of nine attended the investigation, including a reporter from Marquette's TV6 News. Four people, among them the reporter, stayed in the ballroom in hopes of seeing a shadow person, while the rest went down to the locker rooms. In the ballroom, John spoke to whatever spirit might be in the room, asking it to do something to demonstrate its presence. As soon as he had spoken the words, the reporter's camera battery died—even though she had just recharged it. John described it as "like somebody had walked over and flipped the switch on [the camera]. The battery was totally drained."

While the reporter changed her camera's battery, the team could hear something "shuffling around" in the nearby restroom and the sound of the stall doors opening and closing. The team decided to check out the noises, and headed toward the restroom. As they approached the doorway, they could see into the room beyond. There, inside the restroom, they witnessed a pair of legs—with no torso attached—walking around in the space. Suddenly, the legs bolted out of the restroom, morphing into a "black, shadowy mass" as the thing flew right in between the shocked team members. The reporter, according to John, "just about dropped her camera and ran out of the building."

The team returned to the ballroom a few minutes later. At the far end of the room, they spotted the shadow being moving around as if it were looking for something or attempting to perform some task. John and the gang tried to draw closer to the shadow figure, but it vanished in the blink of an eye.

Later, the two halves of the investigation team opted to switch places so that John's group would be in the locker room downstairs. The other group had reported hearing strange noises, but hadn't seen anything. During the switch, as John's group walked down the stairs, one of his teammates took some photos. When they looked over the photos after the investigation, they discovered a dark silhouette in the background of one photo. This "shadow person" appeared to be standing inside a doorway at the end of a hallway opposite where John's group had been standing at the time. At first, the team thought they'd simply captured the

Close-up of the shadow figure. Photo courtesy of John Grathoff, Calumet Paranormal.

The photo of a shadow figure captured by John Grathoff and his team at the Calumet Colossseum. Photo courtesy of John Grathoff, Calumet Paranormal.

reporter's reflection in the glass alongside the doorway. Further research demonstrated, however, that even with her camera held on her shoulder, the reporter did not stand tall enough to account for the shadow figure. The dark silhouette was too tall.

Once in the locker room, John's group experienced more strange activity. John knocked out a rhythm known as "shave and a haircut," stopping in the middle of the pattern to ask any presence in the room to finish it for him. The team had recorded the session in case they might catch any EVPs. When they listened to the recording afterward, they heard a knock responding to John's, finishing the pattern he started.

Do ghosts inhabit the Calumet Colosseum? Any building with a long history, like the Colosseum's, certainly has the potential to foster hauntings. And, as the ghost hunters learned through their research, the Colosseum did at one time host a carnival. The whistling ghost could well date back to that era.

Calumet has a long, and often violent, history—from the Copper Strike of 1913-1914, with its tragic climax, to tales of operahouse murder. Whether or not you believe the ghost stories, one fact is disputable. This village has a history ripe with fodder for just such tales. If tragedy and violence give birth to hauntings, then Calumet surely is home to at least a few earthbound spirits.

CHAPTER TWO
LAURIUM

THE MODERN VILLAGE OF LAURIUM SNUGGLES INTO CALUMET, ITS NEXT-DOOR neighbor. The village was incorporated in 1889 as Calumet, but just five years later it was reincorporated under a different name. The village borrowed its new moniker from the Laurium Mining Company, a local copper mining outfit, and the name originated with an ancient mine in Greece. Laurium may have relinquished its original name so that Red Jacket could become Calumet and the newly rechristened Laurium could acquire its own post office, yet the village retains a unique character. Its historic downtown and the nineteenth-century mansions dotting its side streets offer silent testament to its glory days.

Like Calumet, Laurium has shed its dependence on mining—but not its appreciation for history.

A CHECKERED PAST

By 1890, the village soon to be known as Laurium boasted a population of 1,159 residents. By 1895, when the village reinvented itself, the physical size of town had increased six times. On February 28 of that year, Laurium's first postmaster was appointed. African immigrants assisted in the digging of trenches for the village's sewer lines, further enhancing the ethnic diversity of the region. Within a decade, the population had burgeoned to well over 5,000. The explosion of newcomers triggered new problems—namely, crime. Luckily for the victims, in 1903 Laurium got its first hospital.

The year 1908 brought a flurry of burglaries and holdups that left residents in a tizzy. Law enforcement seemed unwilling or unable to stem the tide of crime. Two years later, the population had swelled to over 8,000. And by 1914, a gang of robbers dubbed "highwaymen" terrorized passengers on the streetcars in nearby Osceola. Expansion proved good for the economy, but bad for personal safety.

Hecla Street in Laurium, circa 1914. A streetcar operated by the Houghton County Traction Company traverses the village. Photo courtesy of the Upper Peninsula Regional Digitization Center.

A CHECKERED PAST

Humans weren't the only fugitives on the loose in northern Houghton County, however. In the early part of the twentieth century, Laurium townsfolk fought a guerrilla war against stray cattle, rounding up the bovine criminals by the dozens. Owners of the wayward cows incurred a fine of two dollars a head, a large sum at the time—especially for the farmers who lost a dozen or more cattle! The village brooked no lawbreakers, not even the four-legged kind.

At one point, Laurium boasted its own airport and its own baseball team. Today, the old airport building houses the Bicentennial Ice Arena. Shortly after the nineteenth century turned into the twentieth, the village built the region's first indoor ice rink, the Superior Ice Palace. In 1914, the village hall was spiffed up and rededicated; today, the date on the building reads 1914, even though this wasn't its construction date.

The tiny town of Laurium earned its place in sports history in 1895. George Gipp, aka the Gipper, was born in the village on February 18 of that year. He would die just 25 years later, after developing pneumonia as a complication of strep throat. During his brief life, Gipp earned a reputation as a consummate sportsman, first helping Laurium's baseball team win the Upper Peninsula championships in 1915, and eventually gaining the distinction of becoming Notre Dame University's first All-American player. He achieved that honor in 1920, the year of his death. He's buried in Lakeview Cemetery, near his hometown. Fifteen years later, the village erected a memorial to Gipp, located on the corner of Lake Linden Avenue and Tamarack Street.

Despite the booming population, Laurium never built its own school system, instead relying on schools run by the mining companies. A parochial school cropped up too, but again, this was not a village-sanctioned endeavor. As the mining operations dwindled, so did the population of the Keweenaw as a whole. Laurium suffered the same decline, leading to the closure of its post office on New Year's Eve 1935. By 1980, the

The memorial to George Gipp, located on the corner of Lake Linden Avenue and Tamarack Street. Photo by Lisa A. Shiel.

population was 2,676, but in recent years the numbers have fallen to an estimated 1,967 as of 2012. These days, the town relies on tourism to sustain its economic well-being. But ghosts of the mining days, both physical and metaphysical, still haunt the vicinity.

A CHECKERED PAST

THE CAPTAIN'S HOUSE

On an unassuming street in Laurium sits a house with a tragic and eerie past. Laurium Manor was built in 1906 by the Canadian-born Thomas Hoatson. In 1867, when Hoatson was six, his family relocated to Rockland, in the Upper Peninsula. Three years later, the clan packed up and moved to Calumet, where Thomas's father served as foreman of the Calumet & Hecla mine, holding the position until his death in 1897. Meanwhile, Thomas Hoatson followed his father's career path and accepted a job at C&H right after high school, in 1878. Just eight years later, Thomas married Cornelia Chynoweth, who

Laurium Manor Inn, formerly the Hoatson House built by Thomas Hoatson. Photo by Lisa A. Shiel.

would earn the nickname "dragon lady" due to her collection of dragon figurines.

Hoatson climbed the career ladder at C&H, achieving the position of "captain," a term applied to mine bosses. While at C&H, Hoatson amassed an impressive resume of accomplishments. His involvement proved a key factor in the formation of the Lake Superior & Western Development Co.—later renamed the Calumet & Arizona Mining Co.—which owned and operated a mine in Arizona. Hoatson also served as the director of First National Bank, the second vice president of Keweenaw Copper Co., and the vice president of Keweenaw Central Railroad, Hancock Consolidated Mining Co, and Superior & Pittsburgh Copper Mining Co. As if that weren't enough for one man, Hoatson would

The historical marker at Laurium Manor Inn. Photo by Lisa A. Shiel.

go on to serve as owner, director, or vice president of numerous other concerns in the mining, banking, and railroad industries. He must've eaten his Wheaties every morning!

Not surprisingly, Hoatson's business acumen helped him stack up quite a bankroll and allowed him to live in luxury, in stark contrast to the lifestyle of most mine workers. In 1906, as a gift for his wife, Hoatson purchased a lot in the village of Laurium, demolished the two houses occupying the space, and erected a brand-new home for his wife and six children. The structure would stand at 13,000 square feet and feature 45 rooms, ranking it as the largest mansion in the U.P. After two years of construction, the family moved in to their new house, which would eventually become known as Hoatson Manor. Thomas passed away in 1929, but Cornelia would stay on in their manor, living alone, well into the 1930s. She then lived with relatives until her own passing in 1947.

By all accounts, the Hoatsons were a kind and generous couple. Their wealth permitted them to hire servants, including three maids, a handyman, and a chauffeur. The Hoatsons treated their servants well, and Cornelia even arranged for her maid's niece, and the niece's children, to move to America from Sweden, when the niece's husband turned abusive.

Two years after Cornelia's death, Maynard and Jane Hurlbert bought the Hoatson Manor. They relocated their business, the Thomas Funeral Home, into the first floor of the mansion, choosing to live upstairs. In 1979, in a tragedy rarely spoken of in the Copper Country, Maynard killed his wife and mentally handicapped foster son, then took his own life. Rumors circulated that Maynard had been diagnosed with a serious illness and, feeling helpless to care for his family in his worsening condition, he made the drastic and horrific choice to end all their lives. No one knows for certain what motivated the crime, but it remains a tragic chapter in the area's history.

Over the next decade, the manor would shift hands several times, and be stripped of many of its valuable antiques. In 1989,

David and Julie Sprenger snapped up the property, transforming the once-proud, but now bleak, mansion into a lively bed & breakfast. The Sprengers financed their renovations all on their own, with no government aid. Restored to its former glory, the mansion—now rechristened Laurium Manor Inn—hosts a bevy of guests every summer. In 1994, the manor was added to the National Register of Historic Places. Today, Laurium Manor serves as a cooperating site in the Keweenaw National Historic Park, a large complex of sites scattered across the Keweenaw Peninsula.

GHOSTS OF THE MANOR

Do spirits haunt the old Hoatson manor? Given its long history, including a stint as a funeral home, Laurium Manor seems an ideal candidate for a haunted mansion. And a few folks have reported strange experiences there.

In 2008, three friends—a man and two women—stayed at the bed & breakfast. While her friends were in their room, the lone woman walked into her own quarters. An eerie sensation overwhelmed her, as if she were not alone in the room, and the urge to get out grew intense. Backing out of the room, she paused in the hall. Just then, a low cry echoed from inside her room. Curiosity eventually overwhelmed her fear, and she crept back into the room. A sense of foreboding swept through her, spurring her to leave the room, and indeed, the upper floor of the manor.

A little while later, the young woman ventured back up to her room, hoping the whatever-it-was had skedaddled. In the doorway of her room stood a little girl the woman had never seen before. She asked the girl, "Creepy, isn't it?" To which the girl replied, "Yeah."

The child then walked away.

Since the woman had agreed to meet her friends in a few minutes, she hurried off to her appointment. When she came back later, she hesitated on the stairs landing. A shrill beeping originated from inside her room. Confused by the noise, and overcome by another wave of foreboding, she tiptoed into her room. The noise was emanating from the alarm clock on the bedside table. The time read 2:22 PM. The woman had not set the alarm, but once she turned it off, the room began to feel normal to her again. After that, she suffered no more creepy sensations.

Did a ghost set off the alarm clock? Had the woman and the little girl sensed the presence of a spirit?

As with all ghost stories, answers elude us. But the possibilities tantalize our minds. Any location with a history as long and tragic as Laurium Manor could harbor a few ghosts.

CHAPTER THREE
KEARSARGE

ANYONE DRIVING ALONG THE SPINE OF THE KEWEENAW, ON U.S. HIGHWAY 41, WILL encounter one small community after another. The lineup starts just north of Hancock, on the far side of the Portage Lake Lift Bridge. From there, a visitor drives through village after village—Centennial Heights, Kearsarge, Wolverine, Allouez, Ahmeek, Mohawk—many of which exist today as a smattering of houses clustered around the highway. But these villages got their starts over a century ago, thanks to the Keweenaw's namesake industry.

Copper mining.

Among these villages one can boast of a claim to fame rivaled only by Calumet, the top copper town in the Copper Country. For Kearsarge, an unassuming village nestled along U.S. 41, once hosted two of the top-producing copper mines in Michigan.

A BOOMING HISTORY

In 1867, the village of Kearsarge was settled. The village received its name thanks to a local resident who had served on the *USS*

Kearsarge, a navy sloop. Its boom time wouldn't set in until fifteen years later, but the history of its rise begins a few miles southwest of the village itself, in another settlement known as Osceola, which lay two miles southwest of Red Jacket and Calumet and a little over three miles from Kearsarge.

THE OSCEOLA EFFECT

In 1873, businessmen seeking their fortunes in copper mining organized the Osceola Mining Company with the intent of exploiting the Calumet Conglomerate, the richest copper lode in the Keweenaw. In the same year, the company formed its own railroad, the Hancock & Calumet, to help in their efforts. Four years later, in 1877, the Osceola Mining Company announced the opening of a new mine. The hype that ensued revolved around the claim that the new mine tapped into a new lode—the Osceola Amygdaloid, discovered by Ed Hulbert, who had found the Calumet Conglomerate. But initial claims proved erroneous, and the Osceola lode turned to be nothing more than a southern extension of the Calumet lode.

False hype aside, the Osceola mine became quite profitable, and by the following year the company had churned out nearly three million pounds (or 1500 tons) of copper. The next year, 1879, proved just as productive. One year later, the Osceola Mining Company merged with the Opechee Mining Company, thereby gaining additional access to the Calumet lode via Opechee's neighboring property. The newly combined operations would be christened the Osceola Consolidated Mining Company. The new company would open new mines—the Wolverine in 1881 and the Tamarack in 1882. Wolverine lies adjacent to Kearsarge; Tamarack sits near Lake Linden, along the shores of Torch Lake.

The Osceola may have proved profitable, but a new lode was on the horizon—and it would become the driving force behind one town's fortunes. While Osceola Consolidated kept up its pace of expansion and production, prospectors uncovered a new, even richer lode a few miles away. Discovered in 1882, the Kearsarge deposit would turn out to be the mother lode—the largest vein of copper in the Keweenaw. The lode stretched for at least forty miles along the Keweenaw's spine and extended to depths of up to two hundred feet. Five years after the lode's discovery, the Kearsarge Mining Company opened a mine, and opened the vein. It would bleed copper for years to come, at nearly a dozen mines scattered along the lode, including the Ahmeek, Allouez, Wolverine, Mohawk, Mayflower, and Seneca mines.

Meanwhile, the miners' discontent reverberating throughout the Copper Country did not leave Osceola Consolidated untouched. In 1892, the Osceola mine endured a strike, and two years later the Tamarack mine suffered its own walk-out. But the most devastating event would hit the Osceola in 1895, when a fire broke out in one of the mine's shafts. Two hundred miners were underground at the time. Thirty could not make it out, perishing from smoke inhalation. The Osceola fire stands as the worst mining disaster in the Copper Country. Despite the tragedy, and the ongoing strife with workers, Osceola Consolidated kept expanding.

In 1897, Kearsarge Mining Company joined with Osceola Consolidated. With a mile of unexploited territory in the Kearsarge lode, the merger gave Osceola Consolidated plenty of fertile ground in which to grow its wealth. In the same year, the company also swallowed up the Tamarack Junior and Iroquois mines, gaining two thousand acres of mineral-rich lands. In 1899, the company opened a second mine at Kearsarge, the South Kearsarge, and the original mine became the North Kearsarge. Thanks to these acquisitions and expansions, Osceola Consolidated, like other copper mining outfits in the region, began paying out substantial dividends to its investors.

By 1903, Osceola Consolidated ranked as the third-highest producer of Michigan copper, after Calumet & Hecla (C&H) and the Quincy Mining Company, both of which worked the Calumet Conglomerate. The following year, in 1904, Osceola

Consolidated bumped Quincy out of the number two spot. Only C&H out-produced Osceola Consolidated. Five years later, perhaps spurred by the competitive spirit, C&H bought out Osceola.

Although the Calumet Conglomerate lode ranks as the highest-producing copper vein in Michigan, the Kearsarge lode held its own. Between the years 1887 and 1925, the North and South Kearsarge mines spit out over 276 million tons of refined copper. From 1882 to 1925, the entire lode amassed a total of nearly 1.2 billion tons of refined copper. The Calumet Conglomerate produced nearly 3 billion tons between 1866 and 1925, placing it firmly in first, and no other lode besides the Kearsarge managed to surpass the billion-ton mark during that period. The third highest producer in the Keweenaw, the Baltic lode, eked out a measly 873 million tons by comparison.

After the tragic miners' strike of 1913-1914, the copper companies fell on hard times. The north end of the Calumet Conglomerate was barren, as were the north and south extensions of the Kearsarge. By 1923, things had gotten so bad that a drastic decision was made. Most of the copper producers in the Keweenaw would merge to form one conglomerate. Thus, the C&H combined with the smaller companies, merging the mines at Osceola, Kearsarge, Ahmeek, and Centennial into one company known as the Calumet & Hecla Consolidated Copper Company. Though mining would continue in the region into the 1960s, by the 1930s the Kearsarge and Osceola mines had shut down.

The Kearsarge lode may have tapped out, but the village would endure.

KEARSARGE, AHOY!

Today, Kearsarge is a quiet town along U.S. 41 that many tourists probably drive through without stopping. The area does boast a Kearsarge-related monument, however it lies in the neighboring village of Wolverine. Since the towns essentially blend into one another, especially for anyone whizzing past on the highway, the distinction may seem trivial. Still, it's a bit odd that the memorial to the *USS Kearsarge*, namesake of the village, technically lies in Wolverine.

Anyone who passes through the twin villages will spot this notable landmark—a stone boat rising out of a cement foundation as

The USS Kearsarge memorial in Wolverine. Photo by Lisa A. Shiel.

A BOOMING HISTORY   41

Sailors prepare for inspection aboard one incarnation of the USS Kearsarge, circa 1890s. Photo courtesy of the Library of Congress, Prints & Photographs Division, LC-DIG-det-4a14296.

if swept up on an earthen wave. Metal gun turrets stand aimed at the highway. Visitors who pull over for a closer look will find a series of plaques explaining the origins and purpose of this boat. The stone boat serves as a memorial to the four U.S. Navy ships christened *USS Kearsarge*. The town earned its name from the first *Kearsarge*, a ship that in turn got its name from Mount Kearsarge in New Hampshire. So in essence, the Michigan village is named after a New Hampshire mountain.

The original *USS Kearsarge*, constructed and launched in 1861, was commissioned by the navy in 1862. The sloop became well-known for the battle its crew fought in France against the *CSS Alabama*, a Confederate ship, during the Civil War. The *Kearsarge* and its crew emerged victorious. After the war, the ship served for many years, protecting American interests in regions as far-flung as the South Pacific and Chile. In 1894, however, the *Kearsarge* ran aground on a reef and sank. All crewman on onboard survived, but the ship was in ruins. Three more *Kearsarge*s would serve the navy, and set out on missions during various conflicts. The fourth *Kearsarge* still serves on active duty today.

The *USS Kearsarge* memorial stands as a testament to both the hardy ships known by that name and the equally hardy men who served on those vessels. Between 1933 and 1934, local men hired by the Works Progress Administration built

The Mohawk Stamp Mill, another remnant of the mining past located just outside Kearsarge. Photo by Lisa A. Shiel.

the memorial, constructing if from cement, mine rock, and—naturally—Jacobsville sandstone. The *Kearsarge* memorial is actually one of three stone boats erected by the WPA at locations around the Copper Country. One of the boats has crumbled away, and a second floats in a grassy field as if it drifted off course and ran aground there.

The third, the *Kearsarge* memorial, sits firmly rooted in a cement foundation. The plaques situated behind the stone boat,

The old Centennial Mine, one of many lodes in the Copper Country, sits just outside Kearsarge. Photo by Lisa A. Shiel.

mounted on a cement wall, honor local veterans and tell the tale of the memorial's origins, as well as the four lives of the *USS Kearsarge*.

Poke a little deeper into the environs of Kearsarge village and we find blocky houses built by the mining companies to house workers, many of them still occupied today. One house in particular accommodates not just the current, living residents, but also a few residents of the ghostly variety.

PHANTOMS OF A BOOM TOWN

The old mining house sits in the village of Kearsarge. A woman—let's call her Jane—who used to live in the house tells of bizarre occurrences, experienced by both her family and the current residents of the home. In the summer of 1990, Jane and her husband bought the house and moved in with their two young children, but the story really kicks off a few years later.

After living in the house for four years, Jane and her family began to hear odd bumps and thumps originating from the upstairs bedrooms. When family members investigated the sounds, they invariably discovered no one upstairs and no source for the noises. Eventually, Jane's daughter started complaining that items were disappearing from her bedroom. A bit of jewelry, a book, loose change or dollar bills—incidental items kept vanishing from the daughter's room, only to reappear at a later time. When the items returned, they would turn up lying in locations where nobody could fail to see them, such as on the girl's bed or on her dresser.

Then things got weirder. Jane's daughter reported being awoken in the night by her TV and radio turning on by themselves. The TV had an old-fashioned knob that must be pushed to turn on the power. Matters escalated from there, and soon the whole family experienced the inexplicable happenings. Often Jane's daughter would go out with friends at night, leaving the

PHANTOMS OF A BOOM TOWN

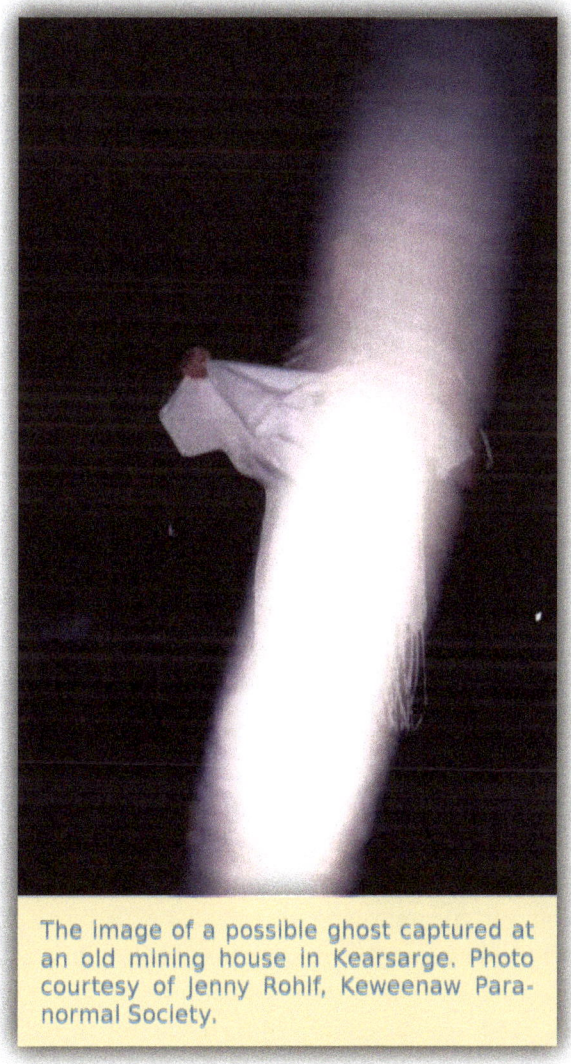

The image of a possible ghost captured at an old mining house in Kearsarge. Photo courtesy of Jenny Rohlf, Keweenaw Paranormal Society.

rest of the family at home. While watching TV in the living room, downstairs, the family would hear the TV or radio in the daughter's bedroom turn on, though they knew the upstairs was vacant. Whenever this happened, they would all exchange mystified looks and say, "What, this again?"

Soon Jane began to experience other phenomena she couldn't explain. Downstairs, she would find water taps in the kitchen and bathroom turning on by themselves. She'd hear bumping and knocking noises in rooms she knew to be unoccupied. On her daughter's thirteenth birthday, during a party held at the house, Jane took a photo of her daughter holding up a T-shirt she'd just received as a gift. Though she saw nothing at the time, after the photo was developed Jane noted a white, swirling fog on the image, almost like a vortex. Skeptics dismiss such things as digital camera artifacts, but Jane had taken the photo with an old 35mm camera. Jane came to believe the photo captured a ghost's image.

In 1999, now divorced, Jane sold the house and moved to a neighboring town. The new owner rented the house to various tenants over the years. Years later, while at work, Jane stuck up a conversation with a co-worker—also named Jane, so let's call her Jane B—who showed Jane A photos of her children. The background of the photos looked familiar to Jane A, so she asked Jane B where her family lived. To Jane A's surprise, she learned that Jane B and her family lived in the old mining house once owned by Jane A and her husband. Jane A didn't mention the paranormal strangeness at the house, but a few days later, she finally did ask Jane B if she or her family had experienced anything. Jane B's eyes widened and, with an air of relief, she rattled off a list of weird and unexplained occurrences she and her family had experienced at the house. Bangs, knocks, disembodied footsteps—Jane B recounted all these things to Jane A. And then Jane B launched into an even stranger story.

One day while her children were at school, Jane B decided to do the laundry. The washer and dryer were down in the basement, so when Jane B needed to put in another load, she had to go down the stairs, leaving her toddler daughter sleeping in a crib upstairs. As Jane B hefted the wet clothes out of the washer, tossing them into the dryer, she heard something upstairs. It sounded like footsteps pounding across the upstairs floor, as if someone were running around in the room above her head. Worried her daughter had escaped the crib, Jane B dropped the laundry and raced upstairs. Her daughter lay sleeping in the crib, oblivious of the pounding noises Jane B had heard a moment earlier. Since Jane B and her daughter were alone in the house, she could find no explanation for the pounding footfalls.

The incident disturbed Jane B so deeply that she immediately began searching for another house to rent. Not long after confiding the story to Jane A, Jane B moved her family to Laurium. Later, Jane B met the man who lives next door to Jane A and, eventually, the couple got married. Now Jane B, who previously lived in Jane A's old haunted house, lives in the house next door Jane A, married to her neighbor. Did their shared paranormal experiences bond the women, or did—unbeknownst to either of them—they share a metaphysical bond before they'd ever met? The coincidences are eerie. Both women share the same first name, worked at the same place, lived in the same old mining house, and experienced similar bizarre happenings in that house. Then they wound up living next door to each other.

Jane A mentions one further tidbit that may have relevance to the hauntings at the old mining house. While living in the house, Jane and her husband remodeled their daughter's bedroom. In the process, they tore out the plaster on the walls in order to put up new drywall. There, hidden beneath the plaster, they discovered drawings of circular patterns and humanoid stick figures. To Jane, the images looked almost ritualistic. Later, after the hauntings, Jane wondered about those drawings. Were they simply doodles scrawled there by a child, or did they have a more sinister origin? No one can say for certain.

So if you drive through Kearsarge, keep one thing in mind. Among all those humble square houses arranged along the highway lies one very spooky residence. Perhaps the ghosts of miners, the past residents of those houses, have clung to their old homes even after death. Perhaps the *USS Kearsarge* memorial attracts the spirits of long-gone navy men. Answers may prove elusive, but the eerie tales told by residents of the old house keep the mystery alive.

In Kearsarge, remnants of the past—whether dilapidated houses or spirits of the dead—hold vigil day and night.

CHAPTER FOUR
JACOBSVILLE

EVERYONE WHO VISITS THE KEWEENAW HEARS ABOUT COPPER MINING—AFter all, the region is nicknamed the Copper Country. But though the Keweenaw is most famous for its copper, one small section of the region produced another highly valued red rock.

Sandstone.

As a sedimentary rock, sandstone consists of sand grains compressed into layers of rock. Jacobsville sandstone, named after the town where quarrying began, comes in two varieties. The pure red sandstone layer lies underneath the so-called raindrop sandstone, which includes bubbles and streaks of white rock. Jacobsville sandstone dates back about a billion years, making it some of the oldest rock in the world. The sandstone layer extends far beyond the limits of the Jacobsville area, even rising up to form cliffs along the Pictured Rocks National Lakeshore near Munising, east of Marquette.

The rock from Jacobsville quarries was used in buildings as far away as New York City, where the façade of the Waldorf Astoria Hotel includes the red stone from Michigan, and even

Montreal in Canada. Many buildings in the Keweenaw also incorporated Jacobsville sandstone into their structure as well, including the Calumet Theatre.

A ROCKY PAST

The area today known as Jacobsville sits one mile east of the Portage Lake Lower Entry—once known as White City—the spot where the Portage River meets Keweenaw Bay. The bay itself forms part of Lake Superior, the largest, deepest, and northernmost of the Great Lakes. Near Jacobsville, on both sides of Portage River, sandstone cliffs plummet down to the waters in sheer drop-offs that, during the spring melt, often produce stunning waterfalls visible from the beach at White City, over half a mile away.

Jacobsville sandstone lines this hidden beach on the shore of Lake Superior, on the Keweenaw's eastern side. Photo by Lisa A. Shiel.

A ROCKY PAST

When explorers first came to the this region, no one yet knew of its copper riches, or of the valuable sandstone beneath their feet. Michigan's first state geologist, Douglass Houghton, embarked on multiple expeditions to the Upper Peninsula, and visited the Keweenaw Peninsula more than once, beginning in 1831 (before he became state geologist). During his 1840 expedition, Houghton remarked on the high quality of the sandstone in the region that would later become known as Jacobsville—and would later fall within the boundaries of a new county named after the state geologist, and which to this day is known as Houghton County. Douglass Houghton thought the area's sandstone would one day prove a valuable commodity. Two decades would pass before anyone took up the task of making Houghton's prediction come true.

Before the advent of sandstone quarrying in the region, the Portage Entry gained its first lighthouse, thanks to the copper industry already booming along the Keweenaw's spine. Ransom Shelden, one of the Keweenaw's industrial pioneers, had lobbied for a light station at the Portage Entry, to help ships transporting copper find their way to and from the area. Shelden got his way, and the first lighthouse at the Portage Entry, a 39-foot free-standing tower, was built in 1855. the lighthouse sat atop a bluff overlooking Keweenaw Bay, with a natural rock foundation as the only separation between the structure and the volatile waters below. The following year, in 1856, the first keeper took command of the light.

Around 1861, an English immigrant named George Craig came to the Keweenaw—specifically, to the area on the east end of the Portage River. Craig had first come to America in 1854, first stopping in Marquette, where he worked as a stone mason, before eventually settling at the Portage Entry. Like Houghton, Craig recognized the value and quality of the sandstone he discovered lying abundant along the shores of the Portage Entry and Keweenaw Bay.

Meanwhile, in 1869, the Portage Entry lighthouse underwent a major rebuilding. Due to structural problems with the original tower, the light was demolished and replaced with a brand-new structure, a 65-foot tower with an attached keeper's residence. The next year, the new light went into operation.

At the same time in 1869, Craig sent samples of his rock, in those days often called redstone, to Chicago in an effort to drum up demand for it as a building material. When those efforts paid off, Craig immediately purchased land in the area, a property that included a good candidate for a sandstone quarry. Ransom Shelden had first acquired the property from the U.S. government in 1854; Craig would turn it into a sandstone quarry, later adding onto his holdings by purchasing more farmland. Thus began the Keweenaw's sandstone industry.

Why then does the area Craig first exploited bear someone else's name? The answer is simple. A man named John Henry Jacobs would become synonymous with the region's sandstone quarrying. Jacobs came to the Portage Entry area around 1861, but when George Craig suffered financial difficulties that forced him to sell out of his quarrying operations, Jacobs bought Craig's quarry. In 1878, Craig switched careers to become the sixth keeper at the Portage Entry light, a post he would occupy for ten years. Meanwhile, Jacobs opened his first venture in 1883, known as the Portage Entry Redstone Quarry. The company would become the first of several quarry operations that to bring Jacobs success—and lead to his name finding its way onto maps.

The quarrying operations attracted many immigrants to area, especially the Finns, whose heritage has played a key role in shaping the culture of the Keweenaw. But Finns were not the first people to chisel valuable rock from the earth around Jacobsville. During the 1885 season, quarry workers unearthed evidence of ancient copper miners in the form of axes, spears, knives, and similar copper implements. No one knows if the ancient miners lived there, or simply discarded their tools in

The Lutheran chapel at Jacobsville still exists today, and services are held here during the summer. The chapel is a historic landmark. Photo by Lisa A. Shiel.

the area. No remains of the ancient miners turned up, but three years later, workers did uncover the skull and femur belonging to a member of a local Indian tribe, whose body had been interred in 1818. These were apparently the only human remains discovered during quarrying. Many workers, however, died or were injured during the quarrying operations. As with the copper mining going on simultaneously elsewhere in the Keweenaw, sandstone quarrying proved a dangerous occupation.

It also proved highly profitable, at least for the quarry owners. The outfit begun by John Henry Jacobs would go through several iterations, as Jacobs changed partners and the company changed names. In the 1887 season alone, the Jacobsville quarries shipped out over fifty thousand tons of sandstone. Though population estimates for the period are hard to come by, and often contradictory, it seems likely that upwards of a thousand people lived in the Jacobsville area during the latter part of the nineteenth century and into the early twentieth century. Other communities cropped up around the quarries to, among them Redrock, Sandstone, and Craig. The latter settlement was named after George Craig, though the lucrative rock he first exploited would bear another man's name, becoming known as Jacobsville sandstone. In fact, the geologic formation that holds the sandstone is known as the Jacobsville formation.

Jacobsville would, by 1887, boast three one-room schoolhouses, a resident doctor, two post offices, a saloon, a justice of the peace, four stores, and a Lutheran church. In 1888, the area received telephone service and gained a wagon trail connecting the settlements to Lake Linden, about twelve miles to the northwest. By 1902, John Henry Jacobs sold his stake in the Jacobsville quarries, but operations would continue without him.

This automated lighthouse stands at the end of a concrete breakwater attached to the beach where White City once was. Photo by Lisa A. Shiel.

Due to the sizable population of the Jacobsville area, a nearby beach had become quite a popular destination for those seeking recreation—and not just the quarry workers found respite there. The popularity of the location led to the inception of a genuine resort. The location, adjacent to the Portage Entry, would in 1907 be christened White City. The man who founded took command of the resort, George Hocking, chose the name because he intended to paint every building in the resort bright white—and he did. The 80-acre resort would eventually feature a pavilion, an icehouse, and cabins, plus additional accommodation in the form tent-houses constructed from wood and tent material. A combination saloon-hotel served guests as well, and an in-house power plant generated enough juice to power up to six thousand electric lights. Steamer ships ferried visitors between Houghton and White City.

By the early twentieth century, sandstone had fallen out of favor as a building material. The quarries would eventually close, and gradually the Jacobsville area would dwindle. Strawberry growing took over as the main product of Jacobsville and the surrounding areas, including those across the bay, leading to the creation of the Copper Country Strawberry Growers Association in 1936—but even that didn't last forever. These days, strawberry growing is mostly associated with the town of Chassell, directly across the bay from White City, where the annual Copper Country Strawberry Festival (begun in 1946) pays homage to the crop that once bolstered Jacobsville's economy. Today the old White City resort has vanished, leaving behind a beach generally referred to as White City, though the only real structure standing on the former resort site is the current lighthouse, an automated beacon constructed in 1920 that sits at end of a long concrete breakwater. In summer, residents still flock the White City beach, though not in the numbers once seen.

Jacobsville has virtually disappeared too, though it left more remnants than White City. The old Lutheran church stands as a historical landmark, with services held there in the summer.

The old schoolhouse, built in 1931, serves as a community center in the summer. A small number of residents live here year-round, with summer folk increasing the population a bit. Some of the old quarries are still visible as ponds, though most lie on private property now. The 1869 lighthouse has gone into private hands as well, operating now as a bed and breakfast.

The heyday of Jacobsville may have come and gone, but some of the old residents have refused to leave—even after death.

SPIRITS OF THE PAST

Given the dangers of sandstone quarrying, we should not be surprised to find spirits haunting areas around Jacobsville. Might some of the ghosts belong to quarry workers? Might others come from the period after the quarries closed, when farmers struggled to make ends meet? Still others may have haunted the region since before Europeans first settled here. Whatever their origins, modern-day residents of the Jacobsville area report strange encounters.

Today, Jacobsville is woods. State land takes up a sizable chunk of the forest north of Jacobsville, as well as a second section along the White City beach. The woods extend right up to the beach, and trees have grown in where buildings and quarries once stood throughout the area. Only remnants of these past activities remain. Yet old farmhouses still dot the forest, reminders of another chapter in Jacobsville's past—the strawberry industry.

THE OLD STRAWBERRY FARM

On one of these old strawberry farms, a few miles from Jacobsville proper, past residents seem unwilling or unable to vacate the premises. A living resident of the home has experienced several ghostly encounters.

The resident had awoken one morning and walked into another bedroom to go into the walk-in closet and get some clothes. The far wall of the bedroom featured two windows that overlooked the nearby woods, and the first morning sunlight shined into the room. The bedroom lay on the second floor of the two-story farmhouse, directly across from the stairs and directly above the living room. This old house has such thick wood

The woods near Jacobsville. Photo by Lisa A. Shiel.

beams in its structure that it's difficult to hear noises from the living room while inside the bedroom, despite its location immediately above the downstairs room. The resident's husband was in the living room at the time, and the TV was on but not playing loudly. As the woman entered the bedroom, she began to hear an odd sound. As clear as any voice she'd ever heard, a man's voice hummed a familiar tune—the old standard "Fly Me to the Moon." The disembodied voice sounded cheerful, and the woman did not feel threatened by the voice, though she was naturally spooked by the experience itself. Where had the voice come from?

She rushed downstairs to tell her husband about the strange humming. He had not been humming in the living room. The TV, though on at the time, was tuned to a news channel that had not featured music of any kind. No commercial had produced the humming. Besides, the upstairs bedroom is well insulated from noises below.

On another occasion, the wife was sleeping in another bedroom when something even spookier happened. She had just begun to wake up and still had her eyes closed, soaking up the faint sunlight that streamed through the windows. After waking, she often lay in bed for a short time in order to let her senses come to full awareness gradually and her eyes adjust to the light. On this particular morning, as she lay there in a wakeful but resting state, all of a sudden she felt someone touch her shoulder. She thought nothing of the gentle touch, since her husband, who rose earlier than she did, often came to wake her so she didn't sleep too late. But then a strange voice asked, "Where's the phone?" Startled, the woman opened her eyes to look at the speaker.

No one was there.

Another time, the wife was again lying in bed letting herself come fully awake slowly. As she lay there, she felt someone kiss her gently on the lips. She thought it must be her husband, but when she opened her eyes, the room was empty. Her husband could have snuck into the bedroom, kissed her, and snuck back downstairs so quickly and without making a sound.

But the paranormal goings-on in this old farmhouse don't end there.

Once while downstairs, the wife was sitting in the living room watching television with her husband. As usual, he was perusing a magazine, glancing up at the TV every so often but mostly engrossed in his reading. The wife had her attention on the TV, but she often glanced over at the two windows directly across from her chair, beside the TV. Behind her lay the kitchen, which is open to the living room, and beyond that the door to the porch. Perhaps ten feet from the witness, behind her back, the kitchen led into the pantry via an open doorway, although the pantry remained out of view from the living room. To her left, behind her, stood the front door. While looking at the living room windows, she could see reflections from the kitchen behind her and from the area near the front door.

On this evening, she glanced away from the TV toward the two windows. Since the sun had long ago set, the view outside was dark and she could clearly see on the glass reflections of the kitchen behind her, as well as the area inside the front door to her left. As she looked at the reflections, the figure of a woman in a long white dress appeared by the front door. Confused, the wife stared at the reflection as she tried to figure out what the humanlike outline might be. As she watched, the ghostly figure walked into the kitchen, straight into the pantry and out of sight. When the witness turned around to check for a prowler, she found an empty kitchen and pantry. She could find no explanation for the figure she had seen, which had looked exactly like a woman in a long white dress.

Other strange occurrences, similar to the poltergeist phenomenon, have also occurred in the old farmhouse. A magnetic thermometer had been placed on the pipe that connects the wood stove in the kitchen to the chimney. One morning, the thermometer suddenly fell to the floor. The magnet still worked, and nothing had disturbed the thermometer—at least nothing of this world. Another time, a boot was moved from the kitchen into the porch. Though no one witnessed the move, the living residents swore none of them had touched the boot. One day it was sitting next to the wood stove, drying, and a little while later it had moved into the porch.

THE SPURNED HUSBAND

A sort of local legend in the Jacobsville area revolves around the disappearances of three people decades ago, probably during the 1940s. Apparently, a man came home one night to find his wife in bed with another man. No one saw any of the three after that night, which of course led to rumors of a double murder and suicide, with the jealous husband as the perpetrator.

Over the decades, residents of the area have reported seeing the figure of a man, always dressed in a plaid shirt and jeans, walking along the roads near Jacobsville. The mysterious man bears a striking resemblance to the jealous husband and never seems to age, lending credence to the idea of murder-suicide and subsequent ghostly manifestation. Was this the unknown figure the ghost of the jealous husband, who had done himself in after fatally punishing his wife and her lover?

Some forty years after the disappearances, a visitor traveling to a relative's house near Jacobsville spotted the plaid-shirted man walking down the road. The visitor stopped to ask the man for directions, and the stranger obliged him. As the visitor drove away, he looked in his rearview mirror but saw no trace of the helpful stranger. On another occasion, a woman encountered the ghost outside a sauna, greeted him cheerfully, and then watched as the ghost vanished in front of her.

HAIRY GHOSTS

Along the beach at White City, where once an extravagant resort teemed with tourists, not much happens these days. In summer, especially on hot days, people still crowd the beach—but the crowds are considerably smaller than in the old days. On one side of the concrete breakwater, pleasure boats and the occasional fishing vessel rumble down the Portage River, aka the canal. The lighthouse built in 1920 flashes its beacon at night, and on foggy days the light is accompanied by the mournful bellow of the fog horn. The fog can lend the beach and adjacent woods an eerie quality.

One visitor to the White City beach reported seeing something even spookier than fog-laden trees, however. A man exploring the vicinity of the beach said he glimpsed semi-transparent figures roaming the area. The figures looked humanoid in shape, if quite tall for a man, but with one major difference—they were covered in hair. The witness felt there might've been undiscovered burial grounds nearby, and that these ghostly Bigfoot originated there.

The Copper Country does have a history of Bigfoot sightings. From Dollar Bay to Mohawk, and Jacobsville to L'Anse, regular folks have reported seeing hairy, bipedal creatures. Any such creature would have to leave behind remains of their dead. The lack of Bigfoot bones has led skeptics to dismiss their very existence as impossible. However, if the White City witness is correct, then Bigfoot bones may be hidden right under our noses.

Wherever the hairy spirits came from, they add another dimension to the paranormal events in the Jacobsville area.

Do ghosts of hairy beasties haunt the beach near White City? Photo by Lisa A. Shiel.

Does this image, captured by a game camera, show a spirit orb in the woods near Jacobsville? Photo copyright by Lisa A. Shiel.

SPIRIT ORBS

Another phenomenon often associated with ghosts is glowing orbs or spirit orbs. People have noticed these unexplained balls of light in photographs taken at locations that have a history of ghost sightings, as well as in other areas. The woods around Jacobsville have their own history of glowing orbs. Could these represent the spirits of deceased residents?

At the old strawberry farm mentioned previously, witnesses have seen balls of light on numerous occasions. Once, while walking in the woods with her husband and their dogs, the wife saw an orange ball of glowing light hovering five or six feet above the ground. She estimated the orb was a hundred feet away and approximately the size of a tennis ball. The orb glittered like a disco ball, with a bright rim around it. The woman blinked but the orb was still there, hovering in the woods. After several seconds, the orb moved off to the right, behind some trees.

On multiple occasions, the wife has seen a bluish-white orb hovering outside the yard gate just outside her bedroom window. The orb is visible only from one window in the house. Reflections on puddles have been ruled out, since the orb has appeared on cloudy and moonless nights. As yet, no reasonable alternative explanation has been found for the mysterious glowing balls witnessed on the property.

A forester working in the area also reported seeing glowing orbs in another section of the woods around Jacobsville. At first, he took the orbs for flashlights, but further investigation revealed no other human presence in the vicinity. Are these orbs UFOs or spirits? In either case, they remain unexplained to this day.

The haunted woods of Jacobsville retain their secrets.

REFERENCES

Many of the stories in this book came out of personal interviews with witnesses and investigators. Other information was gleaned from the following sources:

"Annual Estimates of the Resident Population: April 1, 2010 to July 1, 2012 ." U.S. Census Bureau, Population Division. http://factfinder2.census.gov/faces/tableservices/jsf/pages/productview.xhtml?src=bkmk

Butler, B.S., and W.S. Burbank. *The Copper Deposits of Michigan.* U.S. Geological Survey Professional Paper 144. Washington, D.C.: U.S. Government Printing Office, 1929.

Courter, Ellis W. "Michigan's Copper Country." *Contribution to Michigan Geology*, 92(1), reprinted 2005 by DEQ Office of the U.S. Geological Survey.

Elsila, Dave. "Tragedy at the Italian Hall: Michigan's Copper Country Remembers the 1913 Strike." *Looking Back, Looking Forward: A Newsletter of the Michigan Labor History Soci-*

ety. Spring–Summer 2013. http://mlhs.wayne.edu/files/130509_newsletter.pdf

"Geologic Formations: Pictured Rocks National Lakeshore." National Park Service. Accessed 4 April 2014. http://www.nps.gov/piro/naturescience/geologicformations.htm

Goings, Aaron, and Gary Kaunonen. "Strike! New Perspectives 100 Years Later." *Michigan History,* 97(3).

"Haunted Copper Country 2007." *Houghton Daily Mining Gazette.* 27/28 October 2007.

"Helena Modjeska and the Calumet Theater." Most Haunted Places in America. Accessed 12 November 2013. http://www.ghosteyes.com/helena-modjeska-calumet-theater

"Industrial Calumet: A Guide to the Calumet & Hecla Copper Mining Company Industrial Site." National Park Service. Accessed 12 May 2014. http://www.nps.gov/kewe/planyourvisit/upload/Industrial-Calumet-for-web.pdf

"An Interior Ellis Island." Houghton: Michigan Technological University. Accessed 4 April 2014. http://ethnicity.lib.mtu.edu/index.html

"Jacobsville Sandstones." Copper Country Explorer. Accessed 4 April 2014. http://www.coppercountryexplorer.com/2012/02/jacobsville-sandstones/

"Kearsarge, Michigan." Wikipedia. Accessed 1 July 2014. https://en.wikipedia.org/wiki/Kearsarge,_Michigan

"Kearsarge." Hunt's Guide to Michigan's Upper Peninsula. Accessed July 1, 2014. http://hunts-upguide.com/kearsarge.html

Kleen, Michael. "Top 10 Most Haunted Theaters in the Midwest." Mysterious Heartland, 12 May 2014. http://mysteriousheartland.com/2014/05/12/top-10-most-haunted-theaters-in-the-midwest/

"Laurium Manor Inn Haunting." Community Audio Collection. https://archive.org/details/LauriumManorInnHaunting

Mays, Gabrielle. " Do You Believe in Ghosts?" TV6 News, 2 May 2012. http://www.uppermichiganssource.com/news/story.aspx?list=194550&id=749003[11/12/2013 9:44:12 AM]

Mays, Gabrielle. "What Did the Ghost Hunters Find?" TV6 News, 3 May 2012. http://www.uppermichiganssource.com/news/story.aspx?id=749450[11/12/2013 9:43:09 AM]

Monette, Clarence J. *The Calumet Theatre*. Lake Linden: Clarence J. Monette, 1979.

Monette, Clarence J. *The History of Jacobsville and Its Sandstone Quarries*. Lake Linden: Clarence J. Monette, 1976.

Monette, Clarence J. *White City: The History of an Early Copper Country Recreational Area*. Lake Linden: Clarence J. Monette, 1975.

Nordberg, Jane. "This Isn't a Klondike Town Anymore." *Michigan History Magazine*, 84.3 (2000): 10+.

"The Official Website of George Gipp, The Gipper." Accessed 31 August 2014. http://www.cmgww.com/football/gipp/index.php

"Past-E-Mail: Cam Notes: 2003: October: Oct 31-03." Comment by Wms on "Not Forgotten..." by Mary Drew, 31 October 2003. http://www.pasty.com/discuss/messages/1779/2310.html

Rose, Bill. "Jacobsville Sandstone." GeoElements of Michigan's Keweenaw. Accessed 3 April 2014. http://www.geo.mtu.edu/~raman/SilverI/Sandstone/Welcome.html

Russell, Elizabeth, and Rachael Bussert. "Portage Entry Quarries Company Collection MS-053 Finding Aid." Houghton: Michigan Technological University, 23 October 2013. http://www.mtu.edu/library/archives/collections/documents/ms053.pdf

"Sandstone Quarries of the Copper Country." Copper Country Explorer, accessed 4 April 2014. http://www.coppercountryexplorer.com/2009/06/sandstone-quarries-of-the-keweenaw-p1/

Stancher, Craig. "100 Years Young: Calumet Colosseum." *USA Hockey Magazine*, March 2013. http://www.usahockeymagazine.com/article/2013-03/100-years-young-calumet-colosseum

Stonehouse, Frederick. *Haunted Lakes II: More Great Lakes Ghost Stories*. Duluth, Minn.: Lake Superior Port Cities Inc., 2000.

"Theatre History." Calumet Theatre website, accessed 5 May 2014. http://www.calumettheatre.com/about/our-history/

"Tumult & Tragedy: Michigan's 1913-1914 Copper Strike." Michigan Technological University. Revised 1 November 2012. Accessed 16 June 2014. http://www.1913strike.mtu.edu/index.html

"White City." Keweenaw Convention & Visitors Burea. Accessed 4 April 2014. http://www.keweenaw.info/attractions/ghosttowns/285.html

Whitesall, Amy. "Where Hockey Got Its Start." *Michigan History Magazine*, 94(3): 37-42.

LISA A. SHIEL RESEARCHES AND WRITES ABOUT EVERYTHING STRANGE, FROM BIGfoot and UFOs to alternative history and science. She has a master's degree in library science and previously served as president of the Upper Peninsula Publishers & Authors Association. As a fiction writer, Lisa blends her paranormal interests with sci-fi and romance elements to create her own brand of adventure stories. Her fiction works include short story collections as well as the other novels in the Human Origins Series—including *The Hunt for Bigfoot*, *Lord of the Dead*, and *Relic of the Ancient Ones*. Lisa's nonfiction books explore topics as diverse as Bigfoot, evolution, and Michigan's quirky history.

www.LisaShiel.com

www.ingramcontent.com/pod-product-compliance
Lightning Source LLC
Chambersburg PA
CBHW061224070526
44584CB00029B/3976